D1380741

Paul Mellon

A Cambridge Tribute

The
Fitzwilliam
Museum

This book accompanies the exhibition

Paul Mellon: A Cambridge Tribute
held at The Fitzwilliam Museum, Octagon Gallery
12 June – 23 September 2007

First published in June 2007 by
The Fitzwilliam Museum
Trumpington Street
Cambridge
CB2 1RB
Telephone 01223 332 900
Fax 01223 332 923
Email fitzmuseum-enquiries@lists.cam.ac.uk
www.fitzmuseum.cam.ac.uk

Text compiled by Duncan Robinson
Catalogue compiled by Lydia Hamlett
Photography: Andrew Norman, The Fitzwilliam Museum,
and Yale Center for British Art
Project management: Thibault Catrice, Fitzwilliam Museum Enterprises Ltd
Design: Cantellday www.cantellday.co.uk
Printed by Graphicom srl, Vicenza, Italy

For copyright permission, the publisher wishes to thank the Sir Alfred
Munnings Trust by courtesy of Collectors Guild Limited, Tessa Pullan,
Lady Cressida Inglewood, and Yale Center for British Art

ISBN (10) 0-904454-77-0
ISBN (13) 978-0-904454-77-5

Introduction

This tribute to Paul Mellon is timed to co-incide with the centenary of his birth. By bringing together works from his own collection and objects belonging to the Fitzwilliam Museum, it aims to illustrate his affection for Cambridge and the extent to which his experiences of England influenced his activities as a collector. The text which follows consists mainly of quotations from Mr Mellon's own writings; not only from his autobiography but also from some of the many speeches and talks he gave throughout his life. Reserved and private though he was, he chose his words with as much care as the occasions on which he delivered them, and in so doing revealed with extraordinary candour yet lightness of touch a great deal about his *modus operandi*.

I am deeply grateful to John Baskett, co-author of 'Reflections in a Silver Spoon', and to the Executors of Paul Mellon's Estate, for permission to quote from the autobiography. The Executors also gave me access to and permission to quote from a wide range of published and unpublished material. To Amy Meyers and the staff of the Yale Center for British Art I extend both personal and institutional thanks on behalf of the Fitzwilliam Museum. We are grateful also to the Master and Fellows of Clare College for the loan of Tessa Pullan's Head of Paul Mellon and for joining forces with us to mark with appropriate celebrations the birthday itself, June 11 th. My Research Assistant, Lydia Hamlett, has contributed to every stage of the project, from its inception to its installation. Finally I would like to thank all of my colleagues at the Fitzwilliam Museum for their unfailing support over the past twelve years. With the help of our friends we have brought about some notable changes. One friend in particular made much of it possible: Paul Mellon.

Duncan Robinson
Director 1995-2007

Paul Mellon: A Cambridge Tribute

Paul Mellon, Hon KBE, MA, Hon LL.D, FBA was born in Pittsburgh, USA, exactly one hundred years ago. His father, Andrew W. Mellon, has been described as 'the American colossus who bestrode the worlds of industry, government and philanthropy, leaving his transformative stamp on each.' [1] His mother, twenty-four years younger than her husband, was English. They met in 1898 on a transatlantic liner, sailing from New York to Southampton. He was travelling with one of the Mellon Bank's most important clients, Henry Clay Frick, and his wife; she was with her parents, Mr and Mrs Alexander McMullen, who were returning to Hertfordshire at the end of a round-the-world tour. Two years later Andrew Mellon and Nora McMullen were married, and he took his English bride to live in Pittsburgh, the centre of his commercial and industrial empire. The house he bought for her, 5052 Forbes Street, *'was late Victorian and very dark – the halls were dark, the walls were dark, and outside, Pittsburgh itself was <u>very</u> dark.'* [2] A daughter, Ailsa, was born there in 1901 and six years later, Paul arrived, on June 11 th, 1907.

Paul Mellon sitting for his portrait head by Tessa Pullan, c.1984 © Lady Cressida Inglewood

'From 1907 until 1914,' he recalled, *'from my first year to my seventh, my parents spent almost every summer in England, and my sister and I were invariably taken with them. I suppose it was in those summers that I first developed a taste*

for the English countryside, for English houses, English rivers, English parks, English skies, English clouds – and let's not forget English trains – in those days brilliantly and beautifully painted in reds, greens or blues; all the brass and copper which garnished the engines highly polished, all the engines proudly and aristocratically named . . . . From those distant summers I remember huge dark trees in rolling parks, herds of small friendly deer, flotillas of white swans on the Thames, dappled tan cows in soft green fields, the grey mass of Windsor Castle towering in the distance against a background of huge golden summer clouds . . . . somehow at this great distance it all melts into a sunny and imperturbable English summer landscape. There seemed to be a tranquility in those days that has never again been found, and a quietness as detached from life as the memory itself.' [3] The nostalgia of the last sentence was both deliberate and understandable; in 1912 Andrew and Nora Mellon divorced.

Windsor Castle occupied a special place in Paul Mellon's memory. *'A curious thing happened at the end of my parents' six-month stay in England,'* he wrote in his autobiography. *'They found themselves one day with the Dean of Windsor, and it came up in conversation that I had not been baptized. The Dean, horrified that an infant had crossed the Atlantic not having received baptism, offered to perform the ceremony himself in St George's Chapel at Windsor Castle. So, on December 22, 1907, I was baptized in the historic surroundings of this famous building, scene of many royal baptisms, weddings, and funerals . . . . I have always felt conscious of this*

Andrew W. Mellon and Paul Mellon at Cambridge, Degree Day, 1931

*singular privilege, as if the ceremony somehow foreshadowed
my later addiction to English life and English places.'* [4]

From 1921 to 1932 Andrew Mellon served under Presidents
Harding, Coolidge and Hoover as Secretary of the U.S.
Treasury. His son graduated from Choate School in
Wallingford, Connecticut in 1925 and from Yale University in
1929. He was painfully aware of his father's ambition for him to
join the Mellon Bank, and of his own disinclination to do so. He
toyed with the idea of postgraduate study leading to an
academic career, but was swayed by his mother, *'who was
anxious that I should see more of England (and) urged me to
spend a year or two at an English university. Her brother my
uncle Percy was a friend of the tutor at Clare College,
Cambridge, and he offered to arrange for me to go there.*

I found the notion attractive. I liked England, and going to Cambridge would put off the decision about my future for a year or two, so I agreed.' [5]

Peter De Wint,
Clare College from
the Backs, c.1840
From the collection
of Paul Mellon; lent
anonymously

'I arrived at Cambridge in some ignorance of what exactly I intended to do there. Unlike a Yale freshman, one was not taken in hand and put to work. I found I had been allocated attractive rooms in Clare College, looking out on one side of

Old Court, and on the other over the Fellows' garden, the Backs, and the charming, seventeenth-century bridge that spans the river Cam.' [6]

'Once again, I thoroughly enjoyed living in England; and I drank deeply of her scenery, her history, her life, her sport, her beer. I went to lectures, but Tinker and Phelps had spoiled me, and I found Cambridge lectures dull and dry. I read a little, I studied a little, I finally received a B.A. Honours Degree, although what class is highly classified information! In other words, I r-o-d-e constantly, I r-o-w-e-d intermittently, I r-e-a-d a little.' [7]

Paul Mellon's account bears a more than passing resemblance to the gently satirical drawings of Cambridge by Thomas Rowlandson. He was Secretary of the Boat Club for 1930-31, the year in which it celebrated its centenary. He rowed bow in the Clinker 4, 2nd Lent 8 and 2nd 8 in the May races of 1930 and 3 in the 2nd 8 in the Mays of 1931. As a result he got oars in both years. *'Both oars have always hung above the shelves in my library in the Brick House, and among the other satisfactions I get at looking at them,'* he noted in 1992, *'I am pleased to see that my weight has changed hardly at all.'* [8]

As for literary pursuits, the former editor of 'The Yale Daily News' took on the task of editing 'Lady Clare', the college magazine; *'I wrote editorials and poetry for it, encouraged other students to submit articles, made up the dummy, read proof, and saw it through the Cambridge University Press.'* [9] His editorials ranged from mock-heroic to nostalgic, none more

so than his autumnal rhapsody in 1930 with its highly pictorial language describing *'a fleeting half-hour in which life becomes clear, in which its lines, and colours, and depths take on their true values, and tones, and perspectives. One hears so frequently the warning to grasp the pleasures of life at the moment, especially the pleasures of university life since they, like all fine things, last only for the moment.'*[10] His poetry was similarly pensive and well-crafted, if indebted perhaps to Phelps's popular course at Yale on the Victorians:

> As all lovers might
> We talked as lovers talk when first they meet,
> Not sensing yet their ultimate defeat
> Behind a silver arras of delight.[11]

LADY CLARE

* *

MAGAZINE · OF · THE AMALGAMATED·CLUBS OF · CLARE · COLLEGE CAMBRIDGE

*

BOAT CLUB CENTENARY NUMBER

EDITORIAL COMMITTEE

EDITOR . . . . PAUL MELLON
HON. SECRETARY . . . . A. B. CLEGG
ASSOCIATE EDITOR . . . . .E. L. BIRCH

VOLUME · XXV
NUMBER · THREE
* MCMXXXI *
·

Spending the summer vacation in the Mellon Bank had merely reinforced Paul Mellon's reluctance to follow in his father's footsteps. The relief was palpable when he returned to Cambridge in the autumn of 1930, for *'Cambridge I loved, and I loved its grey walls, its grassy quadrangles, St Mary's bells, its busy, narrow streets, full of men in black gowns, King's Chapel and Choir and candlelight, the coal-fire smell, and walking across the quadrangle in a dressing gown in the rain to take a bath. In the winter, it got dark at 3.30, and all winter the wet wind whistled straight down from the North Sea – and on grey days and sunny days, the flat, wide, seemingly unpeopled, limitless fields stretched endlessly away to the north across the mysterious fens. To the east they rolled gently toward Suffolk and lovely Newmarket, its long straight velvet training gallops, its race-course, to me the most beautiful one anywhere.'* [12]

Speaking to the York Gimcrack Club in 1970, Paul Mellon readily allowed that *'Newmarket beckoned to me, and I saw my first* **live** *English race – the Cambridgeshire of 1929. Later I was to admire York, Goodwood, Sandown, Cheltenham, but I still hark back to those long, soft, eminently green gallops stretching to the horizon in the slanting, afternoon sun, and the late October sunlight on the warm yellow stone of the old, high stands at Newmarket.'* [13] It was while he was at Cambridge that Paul

Mellon discovered foxhunting. *'There I hunted regularly with
the Quorn, the Belvoir, and the Pytchley,'* he recalled. He also
began to acquire horses, including *'a lovely chestnut mare that
I named Lady Clare, and she turned out to be a great jumper
and one of my best and favourite hunters. When I returned to
the States, she came, too, and I kept her at Rokeby.'* [14]

In March 1931 Andrew Mellon purchased the four-hundred acre
Rokeby farm near Upperville, Virginia. It was registered in his
son's name but was bought to provide his former wife with a
permanent home, one reminiscent in many ways of the life in

Alfred J. Munnings,
Paul Mellon on
Dublin, 1933
Yale Center for
British Art, Paul
Mellon Collection
© Sir Alfred
Munnings Trust by
courtesy of Collectors
Guild Limited

the English countryside she had forfeited thirty years earlier.
For their son also it seemed likely to provide a country retreat
from that business career which still beckoned in spite of his
resistance. A keen horsewoman, Nora Mellon encouraged her
son's visits along with his newfound enthusiasm for hunting.
She presented him with a big Irish hunter called Dublin,
the horse that, in his own words *'assured my lifelong addiction
to hunting.'*

In 1932 Andrew Mellon was posted to London as the U.S. Ambassador to the Court of St James. Despite their differences, his son was a welcome and frequent visitor. Their attachment to England was one of their many, common traits; 'Nowhere, outside my own country, could I feel so much at home as here,' His Excellency explained to the Pilgrims, the leading Anglo-American society in Britain, on April 14 th, 1932, two weeks after taking office.[15] Paul Mellon could not have demurred. It gave him the perfect opportunity to prolong his own love affair with his mother's native country. Dublin accompanied him and was lodged with 'Squeaky' Honour, a hunting farmer in Gloucestershire. It was *during this visit to England (that) I asked Alfred Munnings to paint a portrait of me on Dublin. We travelled down together from London to Mr Honour's stables to take a look at the horse. I, who was still pretty reserved, said little on the journey, whereas Munnings, apart from being older, was a great extrovert and far from bashful. He was very amusing company. Looking back, I recall that I was probably a little overawed by my bohemian travelling companion . . . .'*

'Munnings went back to Gloucestershire a couple of times to paint the horse, whom, as a knowledgeable foxhunter himself, he admired. He then painted me in his studio in Chelsea. I received a photograph of the finished picture before Munnings had it delivered. Looking at it, I thought the bushy willow tree on the left was a little disturbing and wrote to Munnings asking whether he could do something to make it slightly less prominent. Sometime later I got a blast back saying in the first

place, the tree wasn't a willow, it was a pollarded oak, and second, he had no intention of changing anything whatsoever. So that was that.' [16]

In a talk he gave to a group of his son's friends at Yale in 1964, Paul Mellon opined that *'like so many things in life, you don't see any direct connection between causes and effects or between isolated pastimes, interests, and emotions until years later.'* [17] He went on to explain that it was *'while I was at Cambridge, and a year later while I occasionally stayed in London with my father during his Ambassadorship, I began collecting books, particularly English color-plate books and books on racing and hunting (another unfortunate and expensive habit I have never been able to break). From the Robinson brothers in Pall Mall, I bought my first illustrated sporting book in 1931 – Strutt's Sports and Pastimes of the People of England. Later, after I was first married in 1935, and until World War II, I began buying racing and hunting and other sporting paintings ... My father gave me two of my best Ben Marshalls and two Sartoriuses as wedding presents, although he detested hunting as being very dangerous and racing as being very foolish, and he often said, "Any damn fool knows one horse can run faster than another." It was, however, at about this very time that I bought my first racehorse (an interesting commentary on the influence of parental advice)!'* [18]

Walking along the Cambridge Backs on a spring morning in 1930, Paul Mellon came across *'a Clare man, a rowing friend, who was instructing a group of undergraduates in the manual of arms.'* Perhaps recalling his summer holidays at Camp Marienfeld in New Hampshire where he found that *'being shouted at by an Army officer was far preferable to receiving strictures from a nurse,'* [19] he determined to follow his friend's example by enlisting in the Territorial Army. When he gave his address as Pittsburgh, Pennsylvania, however, the recruiting sergeant turned him away with "We can't give the King's

Shilling to a foreigner. What would happen if there were a war?"[20] That question was answered in due course; after training as a cavalry officer in the United States, Captain Mellon was posted to England in 1943 where he was eventually assigned to the Office of Strategic Services. Sharing a rented house in Belgravia with a fellow officer, he responded with wry humour to wartime London, with its blackout and rationing. One night, he recalled, *'we both decided to stay home for dinner. We discovered a saucepan on the stove with large lumps of meat and some rice in it. We couldn't make up our minds whether it was some sort of soup, to which we were meant to add water before heating, or a stew. Being inexperienced cooks, we filled the saucepan with sufficient water to cover the meat and then heated it over the gas ring until it had boiled a little before serving it up. It had a disgusting taste, and we found we couldn't eat very much ..... The following day the housekeeper looked at us resentfully and said "You absolutely ruined my cat's dinner."'*[21]

At the end of the war, Major Mellon as he was by then returned to the United States to shoulder the burden of his father's legacies: the National Gallery of Art in Washington and a portfolio of charitable foundations which were to be amalgamated in due course into the Andrew W Mellon Foundation. While 'giving away a fortune wisely', as he once described his task, he and his second wife, 'Bunny', began to form that remarkable collection of works by the French Impressionists which they divided, eventually, between the National Gallery of Art and the Virginia Museum of Fine Arts. On the other hand, *'Bunny wasn't interested in British art,'* he

Thomas Rowlandson, The Recruiting Sergeant, c.1790 Yale Center for British Art, Paul Mellon Collection

wrote, *'and looking back, I really needed someone to help get me going. The catalyst that caused me to launch out so suddenly, at the age of fifty-two, came in the form of the art historian Basil Taylor.'* [22] Their meeting took place in 1959 and it is a measure of its impact, of the speed and efficacy of this sudden launch, that five years later, the winter exhibition at the Royal Academy in London, simply but definitively entitled 'Painting in England 1700-1850', was drawn entirely 'from the collection of Mr and Mrs Paul Mellon.'

What is clear from countless anecdotes as well as the autobiography, is the sheer pleasure Paul Mellon and those who advised him derived from their pursuit of the finest examples of British art. They hunted not only along the highways of Bond Street and Madison Avenue but through unfamiliar and often surprising byways; a furniture sale at Harrods for Stubbs' 'Zebra', a polaroid from a lady in Manitoba offering his 'Sleeping Leopard'. Like any sport, this one brought disappointments as well as triumphs, but there were rarely hard feelings when too high a price, or an export ban, deprived the hunters of the prize.

'I don't believe many motives in life are clearcut or self-evident,' he wrote. *'Collecting especially is such a matter of*

George Stubbs,
Sleeping Leopard,
1777
Yale Center for
British Art, Paul
Mellon Collection

time and chance – intellectual bent, individual temperament, personal taste, available resources, changing fashion – and the psychologists tell us, even very early child-training – and my own motives as a collector seem to myself extremely mixed. Although temperamental trends or subjective impulses were perhaps uppermost, I won't say it was done entirely without thought, without reason, without plan. English Art, as well as being personally desirable, seemed to me long neglected or even abandoned, not only in this country but also in its homeland.' [23] To redress the balance in its favour he established the Paul Mellon Foundation in London under the direction of Basil Taylor to encourage a wider knowledge and

appreciation of British art. In 1970 that became the Paul Mellon Centre for the Study of British Art, a charitable foundation under the auspices of Yale University which has during the past four decades worked in close association with the London branch of Yale University Press to transform the scholarship of the subject.

What held true for British art generally applied even more so to sporting art; *'how unfortunate that these great painters, particularly Stubbs, should have been neglected over the years and even up to the present day, by the art world at large, and by your compatriots as well, only because they were considered mere sporting artists,'* Paul Mellon pointed out to his audience at the York Gimcrack Club. *'No other country has produced the wealth and variety of animal and sporting art as has England,'* he continued, warming to one of his favourite subjects. *'How long the list of your own sporting artists – perhaps not all of the first rank as artists; but every one of them interesting or amusing or historically valuable for their preservation of scenes of the times, whether absurd hunting exploits, stately coaches bowling along through sun, rain, or snow, or decisive moments in races long past. How much pleasure they have given to how many people over the centuries. How much poorer in inner vision would we, who inhabit the worlds of racing, hunting, fishing, and shooting be without the amusement and action of Alken, the facility of Ferneley, the homeyness of Herring, the mastery of Marshall, the mellowness of Morland, the prolixity of Pollard, the ribaldry and rascality of Rowlandson, the style and simplicity of Seymour, the*

James Ward,
Theophilus Levett
and a Favorite
Hunter (detail),
1814-18
Yale Center for
British Art, Paul
Mellon Collection

sublimity of Stubbs. All of them have enriched our days on the racecourse or in the hunting field or by the fireside. All of them are essentially and unequivocally English.' [24]

Inclined as he was to think of his collecting of British art *'as the most enjoyable end-product of my Yale and Cambridge education,'* [25] Paul Mellon's appreciation of art was intimately

connected to his knowledge of history and literature. *'I fully appreciate that when one looks at pictures,'* he wrote, *'it increases the pleasure to have an understanding of the social and economic backgrounds of the periods in which they were painted. Other factors, from literary connotations to the history of costume, also play their part.'* On the other hand, he insisted that *'paintings, insofar as they are works of art, stand or fall on their own merits. Richard Wilson in Rome, George Stubbs at Newmarket, J M W Turner in the Alps, or John Constable on Hampstead Heath were, in my view, committing to canvas their wonder at the splendors of nature and at the beauty of light.'* [26] In 1977, at the dinner for the opening of the Yale Center for British Art, he added that *'it is a landscape and a life that is fast disappearing, and these beautiful*

15

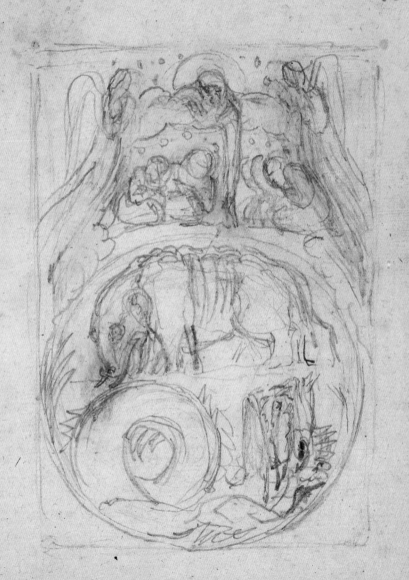

windows on that world may in future years be the only reminders of a world gone by.' Looking today at Constable's treatments of Hampstead Heath and its surroundings, is to be reminded all too vividly of the justice of those words.

Speaking at the dedication of the Paul Mellon Art Center at Choate School in 1972, the donor shared with his young audience some of his thoughts about *'the art experience – whether seeing and hearing or doing and making – (as) a meeting place of thoughts and dreams and feelings. Whatever the inner eye sees within, or the outer eye sees in the outside world, the act of putting it on canvas or paper, or moulding it into a form of plaster, marble or bronze – this art experience, this creative act, provides a meeting ground between thought and experience, dreams and reality, between the psyche and the body, between the conscious and unconscious mind. Happiness is the sensation of the head, the heart, the eyes and the hands all working together toward the same end.'* To illustrate his claim that *'in the assimilation by the individual of the creative visions and concepts of the great artists of the past and present, something new is born in the heart and in the mind,'* he cited the example of William Blake. *'Here was a poet who drew, engraved, painted and brought it all together in his books illustrating his own poems and prophetic verses –*

William Blake,
Sketch for the Book
of Job, Behemoth and
Leviathan, c.1823
The Fitzwilliam
Museum

someone with a highly imaginative intellect – and an
accomplished artist as well. Surely his imaginative gifts came
from a deeper layer of the unconscious than normal.' [27]

Paul Mellon made his first Blake purchase in 1941; the album of
twenty-two watercolour illustrations for the 'Book of Job' which
have since been re-attributed to the circle of John Linnell. He
refused to be discouraged by arguments over their authenticity,
not least because as he explained on more than one occasion, *'I*
have never bought (works of art) as an investment, except as an
investment in pleasure, as treasures to the eye.' [28] Within months,
he acquired a copy of Blake's first Illuminated Book, 'There Is No
Natural Religion', and from then onwards, as Patrick Noon has
pointed out, 'hardly a year passed without Mr Mellon's acquiring
some Blake opus.' [29] Eventually his collection comprised twelve
copies of the Illuminated Books in addition to several hundred
watercolours and prints, and four tempera paintings, including
'The Horse', an illustration for one of William Hayley's 'Ballads',
which was re-issued in 1805. [30] As Noon argues, this
extraordinary collection 'uniquely joins the many strands of Paul
Mellon's private interests and experiences – his passion for books
and for British art.' [31] It is hardly surprising that his enthusiasm
for Blake extended to the works of his followers, among whom
Samuel Palmer stands out for an intensity of vision which owed
so much to Blake. In 1962, Paul Mellon made his first gift to the
Fitzwilliam Museum; the small ink drawing by Palmer of 'Dark
Trees by a Pool' which had belonged to Martin Hardie, the author
of the three-volume history of 'Watercolour Painting in Britain'
which was underwritten by Paul Mellon and published between

William Blake,
The Horse, from
William Hayley's
Ballads, c.1805-6
Yale Center for
British Art, Paul
Mellon Collection

John Constable,
Hampstead Heath
(detail), 1820
The Fitzwilliam
Museum

1966 and 1968. Offering works in Hardie's memory to institutions with significant collections of English watercolours was in itself part of the campaign to stimulate interest in the subject. Rather like the naming of his racehorses, Paul Mellon took particular pleasure in referencing his gifts to people and to places. Thus his gift of Roubiliac's marble bust of Alexander Pope to the Yale Center for British Art was made '*in memory of the British art historian Basil Taylor,*' who not incidentally bore a passing resemblance to the poet, '*friend, mentor, and generous source of wise advice in the course of assembling this collection of British art.*' Similarly, in 1990, he gave three of his unique wax sculptures by Degas to the Fitzwilliam Museum in honour of Michael Jaffé, whom he admired as its director from 1973 to 1990.

On receiving the Hadrian Award from the World Monuments Fund in 1984, Paul Mellon remarked, '*I hope I will not sound ungrateful if I say that awards for patronage have always seemed to me somewhat redundant, since the immediate rewards of patronage are already so great ... I have always thought there are two rewards in collecting – the pleasure of ownership, of seeing paintings and sculptures in the course of one's daily life, and the even greater pleasure of donorship, of seeing them displayed in a public museum.*' [32] Thanks to his extraordinary generosity, that pleasure is now shared by museum visitors world-wide; in Cambridge and London, in Paris, and above all in New Haven, Richmond and Washington DC.

Samuel Palmer,
Dark trees by a Pool,
c.1826-27
The Fitzwilliam
Museum, gift of
Paul Mellon

1   From the blurb to David Cannadine's biography, *Mellon: An American Life*, Allen Lane, 2006.

2   Paul Mellon, *A Collector Recollects*, from a speech delivered at the opening of the exhibition *Painting in England, 1700-1850* at the Virginia Museum of Fine Arts, Richmond 20 April 1963 and published subsequently in *Selected Paintings, Drawings and Books*, Yale Center for British Art, New Haven, Connecticut, 1977, p. v.

3   ibid., pp. v-vi.

4   Paul Mellon with John Baskett, *Reflections in a Silver Spoon: A Memoir*, New York and London, 1992, pp. 38-39.

5   ibid., p. 117. Henry Thirkill (1886-1971) was Senior Tutor at the time; later Master (1939-58).

6   ibid., p. 118.

7   *A Collector Recollects*, pp.vi-vii. Chauncey Brewster Tinker and William Lyon ('Billy') Phelps were both renowned Professors of English literature at Yale.

8   *Reflections*, p. 120

9   ibid., p. 122.

10 *Lady Clare*, vol. xxv, no. 1, 1930, p. 3.

11   ibid., p. 7.

12 *A Collector Recollects*, p. vii.

13 From an address by Paul Mellon at the Two Hundredth Annual Dinner of the York Gimcrack Club, December 11, 1970 (n.p.)

14 *Reflections*, p. 125.

15 Quoted by David Cannadine, *op. cit.*, p. 457.

16 *Reflections*, p.125.

17 mss. Speech at Scroll and Key, Yale University, March 15, 1964.

18 ibid. These remarks were adapted from a speech delivered at the opening of the exhibition *Painting in England 1700-1850* at the Virginia Museum of Fine Arts, Richmond, April 20, 1963, and developed further in *Recollections*, p. vii.

19 *Reflections*, p. 92.

20 ibid., p. 121.

21 ibid., pp. 201-202.

22 ibid., p. 276.

23 *A Collector Recollects*, p. ix.

24 See note 10.

25 *A Collector Recollects*, p. x.

26 *Reflections*, p. 323.

27 mss. Dedication of the Paul Mellon Art Center at Choate School, May 12, 1972.

28 quoted in an article by Paul Mellon which appeared in *Potomac* Magazine, *The Washington Post*, March 13, 1966.

29 Patrick Noon, *The Human Form Divine: William Blake from the Paul Mellon Collection*, New Haven and London, 1997, p.5.

30 Martin Butlin, *The Paintings and Drawings of William Blake*, New Haven and London, 1981, p. 312, no. 366. Butlin places a question mark after the date 1805, adding that 'alternatively the picture may be a later replica of the engraving.'

31 Noon, *loc. cit.,* p.3.

32 mss. Remarks by Paul Mellon on the occasion of receiving the Hadrian Award from the World Monuments Fund, The Plaza Hotel, New York, October 20, 1989.

John Sell Cotman,
The Travelling Artist
(detail), c.1835-40
The Fitzwilliam
Museum

From
Kings College

Catalogue of Works

(in order of their appearance in the exhibition)

Alfred J. Munnings (1878-1959)

Paul Mellon on Dublin, 1933

Oil on canvas, 78.7 x 95.3cm

Yale Center for British Art, Paul Mellon Collection

© Sir Alfred Munnings Trust by courtesy of Collectors

Guild Limited

John Sell Cotman (1782-1842)

The Travelling Artist, c.1835-40

Graphite on pale brown paper, 23.9 x 30.4cm

The Fitzwilliam Museum

Tessa Pullan (b.1953)

Paul Mellon, 1984

Bronze head, height 29.2cm

The Master, Fellows and Scholars, Clare College, Cambridge

John Constable (1776-1837)

Windsor Castle, 1818

Graphite on paper, 10 x 13.2cm

The Fitzwilliam Museum

Two emblazoned Clare College Boat Club oars won
by Paul Mellon, c.1930

Wood, paint and gilding, 20.3 x 386.1 x 30.5cm, each

Yale Center for British Art, Gift of Paul Mellon for the
Founder's Room

William Orpen (1878-1931)

Paul Mellon, 1924

Oil on canvas, 72.4 x 59.7cm

Yale Center for British Art, Paul Mellon Collection

Clare College 2 May Boat, 1930-31

Photograph, 40.6 x 81.3 x 1.3cm

Yale Center for British Art, Gift of Paul Mellon for the
Founder's Room

Peter De Wint (1784-1849)

Clare College from the Backs, c.1840

Watercolour, 47 x 30.8cm

From the collection of Paul Mellon; lent anonymously

Thomas Rowlandson (1756-1827)

West Room and Dome Room, in the Old University Library,

Cambridge, 1800

Graphite, pen and ink with watercolour on paper, 18.9 x 27.5cm

The Fitzwilliam Museum

'Lady Clare' Magazine of the Amalgamated Clubs

of Clare College

Vol. XXV, no. 3, 1931

John Wootton (1678-83-1764)

A Race on the Beacon Course at Newmarket, c.1720

Oil on canvas, 85.7 x 143.9cm

The Fitzwilliam Museum, gift of Paul Mellon

George Stubbs (1724-1806)

Newmarket Heath, with a rubbing-down house, c.1765

Oil on canvas, 30.5 x 40.6cm

Yale Center for British Art, Paul Mellon Collection

George Stubbs (1724-1806)

Gimcrack with John Pratt up on Newmarket Heath, 1765

Oil on canvas, 100 x 124cm

The Fitzwilliam Museum

Thomas Rowlandson (1756-1827)

King's College, and part of Clare Hall, seen from the Backs,

undated, c.1800

Pen, ink and watercolour on paper, 19.8 x 28.5cm

The Fitzwilliam Museum

George Stubbs (1724-1806)

A Comparative Anatomical Exposition of the Structure

of the Human Body with that of a Tiger and a Common Fowl:

Human Skeleton, Lateral View, in a crouching position,

1795-1806

Graphite on thin wove paper, 44.8 x 28.3cm

Yale Center for British Art, Paul Mellon Collection

George Stubbs (1724-1806)

Sleeping Leopard, 1777

Enamel on Wedgwood Biscuit Earthenware, 10.8 x 16.8cm

Yale Center for British Art, Paul Mellon Collection

George Stubbs (1724-1806)

Plate IV, from The Anatomy of the Horse, 1766

Etched plate, 37.9 x 47.6cm

The Fitzwilliam Museum

James Ward (1769-1859)

Theophilus Levett and a Favorite Hunter, 1814-18

Oil on canvas, 99.7 x 130.2cm

Yale Center for British Art, Paul Mellon Collection

John Dalby (op.c.1826-1853)

The End of the Day, 1849

Oil on canvas, 35 x 43.2cm

The Fitzwilliam Museum, bequeathed by Paul Mellon

John Dalby (op.c.1826-1853)

Jumping the Brook, 1849

Oil on canvas, 35 x 43.2cm

The Fitzwilliam Museum, bequeathed by Paul Mellon

Thomas Rowlandson (1756-1827)

A Varsity Trick: Smuggling In, undated

Watercolour on paper, 28.4 x 20.2cm

The Fitzwilliam Museum

Thomas Rowlandson (1756-1827)

The King's Arms, Dorchester, undated

Pen, black ink and watercolour on paper, laid down, 27.4 x 41cm

The Fitzwilliam Museum

Thomas Rowlandson (1756-1827)

The Pursuit, 1808

Pen and ink outline with watercolour on paper, 13.3 x 21.9cm

The Fitzwilliam Museum

Joseph Strutt (1749-1802)

The Sports and Pastimes of the People of England

London 1801

The Fitzwilliam Museum

Sleeping Fox, 1840

Terracotta, 8.8 x 28.5cm

The Fitzwilliam Museum

John Constable (1776-1837)

Hampstead Heath Looking towards Harrow, 1821

Oil on paper laid on canvas, 26.4 x 31.1cm

Yale Center for British Art, Paul Mellon Collection

John Constable (1776-1837)

Hampstead Heath Looking towards Harrow, 1821-22

Oil on paper laid on canvas, 29.5 x 48.3cm

Yale Center for British Art, Paul Mellon Collection

John Constable (1776-1837)

Hampstead Heath, with a bonfire, c.1822

Oil on canvas, 27 x 32.1cm

Yale Center for British Art, Paul Mellon Collection

John Constable (1776-1837)

A View of London, with Sir Richard Steele's House, c.1831-32

Oil on canvas, 21 x 28.6cm

Yale Center for British Art, Paul Mellon Collection

John Constable (1776-1837)

Hampstead Heath, 1820

Oil on canvas, 54 x 76.9cm

The Fitzwilliam Museum

William Blake (1757-1827)

The Horse, from William Hayley's Ballads, c.1805-6

Tempera with pen and black ink on a copper engraving plate,

10.6 x 6.4cm

Yale Center for British Art, Paul Mellon Collection

John Linnell and his Circle (1792-1882)

Illustrations of the Book of Job, pl.16 (page 15):

[Behemoth and Leviathan], 1828

Pen and ink and watercolour, 14 x 10.2cm

Yale Center for British Art, Paul Mellon Collection

William Blake (1757-1827)

Illustrations of the Book of Job, Behemoth and Leviathan,

pl.15, 1825

Engraving with watercolour and wash, 21.3 x 16.4cm

The Fitzwilliam Museum

William Blake (1757-1827)

Illustrations of the Book of Job, Behemoth and Leviathan,

pl.15, c.1823

Graphite and Indian ink on paper, 14.6 x 9.9cm

The Fitzwilliam Museum

Samuel Palmer (1805-1881)

Dark trees by a Pool, c.1826-27

Pen and sepia ink, sepia wash on card, stuck down, 10.5 x 6.7cm

The Fitzwilliam Museum, gift of Paul Mellon

Front endpaper: Clare College, Old Court
Back endpaper: Paul Mellon on 'Lady Clare', c.1931

Paul Mellon with
Mill Reef, Geoff
Lewis Up, Derby
Day 1971